YET
OTHER
WATERS

YET
OTHER
WATERS

WALTER
BARGEN

TIMBERLINE PRESS
1990

The following poems appeared previously in the
indicated magazines, which we thank:

"Yet Other Waters" *The Missouri Review*
"Outage" *River Styx*
"The Collectors," "A Brief Note on Principles,"
and "Relativity" *The Chariton Review*
"Staying in One Place" *Permafrost*

ISBN 0-944048-02-1

Timberline Press
Rt. 1 Box 1434
Fulton, Missouri 65251

Contents

Drinking tea
I tasted the seven seas.

--Shinkiche Takahashi

I sailed in my stones so long
that I became the child
of the five continents.

--Edmond Jabes

The Collectors
for Rod Santos

THIS is drought, and all the sacrifices,
leaving the car windows down, the barbeque
pit open to puddle and rust, the sheets
and pillow cases hanging on the clothesline
mimicking clouds come to rest, or standing
in the yard with or without clothes, any-
thing that might draw rain down, having

given up the turtle shell rattle, the eagle
bone whistle, bare feet moving in circles
and enjoining the desiccated earth to rise
as dust around ankles, the breathing of
a prayer; and still no rain, so we walk
across what water once covered,
the hard crusted sand at the head

of an island, following the splay-toed tracks
of blue herons and the smaller sandpipers,
watching a seagull fly along the distant
cottonwood crowded bank above a wing
dike, where water heaves itself forward
and is shoved back to mid-channel, but is
not enough for stranded barges and towboats

scraping their flat hulls, waiting for
dredges to scoop out the silted-up river-
bed, for one final trip to port to ratchet
steel cables to capstans that will stretch
and snap, and then drift nowhere but down.
At our feet, spreading over this end of
the island and back into the murky water,

are stones polished by the river's tireless
turning, stones rolled and tumbled toward
annihilation, stones so thin they are
nearly transparent and delicate as insect
wings, and among their vitreous shimmer
there are handfuls of petrified wood, bone
fragments, amber, the teeth of extinct bison,
arrowheads and flint chips, stones without
names that have memorized earth's ancient
cracking, their surfaces shrivelled black
and lined with deep creases; this is what
the river leaves, the hard shadows of
water's withdrawing, a rain of stones.

Outage

AS if the sky were stomping
its feet demanding they appear,
they do, with arms folded across
their chests, or hands bulging
in their pockets, suggesting
a need to protect the little
that can't be forgotten
through these hours,
over these years.

They stand, scattered on the loading
dock, drawn from inside a windowless
building by sudden darkness,
and the heavy hammering downpour
on the metal roof. Across the street,
on the otherside of this rain,
they see similar lives surfacing.
Another loose row of men have
gathered, and they wave slowly,
as if the day were now something
less--no softball or mowing grass,
just waiting.

Below the dock, where water pours
from the awning, sawdust from
packing crates turns to mush.
They watch these small, fragile
rafts float down the gutter
to the sewer drain. For a moment
the parked trucks glisten,
as if given a new life,
and the streaks of diesel

exhaust mascara over the rain-
washed cabs, smearing toward
another night.

One Bird, No Stone

for Peter Noce

THE road to the house
follows a razor-back ridge.
On either side creeks meander,
and at odd turns reflect
sheets of rippled light.
He stops the van on a wide
curve before the barn, opens
the door, jumps out without
a word to his passengers,
and runs past the century
walnut that lords over
the pasture, where he was
married a second time.

A squat, balding, and bespeckled
Sicilian with a quartz crystal
and chert arrowhead tied to
a leather cord around his neck,
an angora rabbit vest trailing
heron and crow feathers, red
sweat band around his head,
sandals invisible in the knee-
high grass, all making swift
and elegant moves in erratic
directions across the field
toward a cluster of cedars.
He stops near the fence,
as if coming to the end
of one world, and dives
over the edge leaving
stunned faces in the van.

He reappears holding at arm's
length, upside down by its claws
and struggling, wings flapping
and beak slashing, a wild tom
turkey, whose long stiff beard
hairs he will wear the next day
hanging from his neck, like
a small broom, that sweeps
as he walks, a room no one
else has seen.

Down River

for Jamie

FIRST it was seven then eight geese,
one or another obscured by distance
and shifting positions, theirs and mine,
as they flew upriver in a broken chain,
level with the trees along the bank.

In the middle of a towering cottonwood
a blue heron perched, its questioning
neck and small head rising above
the foliage, as if this is what remained
of thought after so many years

beside this mute, muddy water twisting
toward the gulf. This is what I had seen,
and didn't really have much to say,
wandering barefoot toward her on the steeply
sloping beach cut by earlier reaches

of river. I had just walked the island's
shifting edges, and she was still wet and drying
listening to the current sigh south,
and in that awkward meeting she recalled two
decades, to eighteen and pregnant, parents

pressing for an abortion, and the evening
before going to the clinic, she had stopped
by the house I rented on a street where music
poured out of windows and war was a rumor.
"Did I remember?" I didn't know

what to say, until she mentioned no one

seven

was home, and with her lover she had written
a message on the porch with stones
    from the driveway, that I must have walked
        through with deaf feet, as I did searching

        the island's circumference, finding pieces
    of leaded glass, oddly worn stones, rail
spikes, feathers, all that had washed
    up in wide sweeps of gravel, eroded
        and smoothed until even quartz felt

        as if it belonged in my palms: but not
    a lover. She said it was just
last week, after these many years, that they
    met again: he's off drugs, living
        in a Zen monastary

        in the hills above the river, working
    as a carpenter; and she with one child,
divorced, remarried, teaching art
    part-time. We stood knee deep
        in the water, the wakes of our legs

        trailing ahead as we faced down river,
    current cutting sand from under our feet;
and we squinted at the sun broken across
    the backs of too many waves, before turning
        from this dazzlingly slow sinking.

eight

On Petite Saline Creek

A thin line of dark mud
    marks the edge of near-
        stagnant water, and from
    there up the steep bank
is cracked and pale,
    unaccustomed to so much
        light. A few grasses

venture down this far,
    then yellow as the creek
        slips lower. Swallows
    swirl the turgid surface,
plunging from high-maple
    branches into arcs
        around half-submerged

logs that jab through
    the glistering and twist
        into the air.
    All this aerial display
for a swarm of slender-bodied
    mayflies, whose lives are
        too hurried for eating,

lasting the light of one summer
    day; a life of fluttering
        grace and absence,
    even with the snapper
that drifts past, clouded
    with flies, its legs
        and neck stiffly

pointing away from the belly-
up carapace. We hold our
breaths and pass
quickly, drawing near
a heron that flies downstream
with widening wingbeats
awakening the air

before vanishing beyond
the next bend. We must choose
channels carefully, between
water-logged shadows
and sagging sycamores.
Canoe and paddles
stir murky water,

bubbles percolate and linger
before breaking,
and the needle silhouettes
of gar are stitched just
below the broken glare
of sunlight; it's here
we turn back,

an awkward syllable
that will not drown
or dissolve in the creek's
constricting throat, where
the heron calmly glides over the trees
into riverbottom fields
and we head upstream,

paddling hard, without the assurances
of obols under our tongues,
without a silent stranger

to pry open our hardened
mouths, and guide us
between clay banks
past the turtle's

bloated clarity and our
uncertainity of where
we left off, or where
we might start again, before
those gods fallen under worlds
rise to the small salt
of this one.

Chicken Little Revisted

I saw two men carrying
    a piece of sky under
        their arms, nothing

mythic or legendary,
    simply workers in
        baggy, paint-stained

overalls, sleeveless t-shirts,
    and small white caps that
        displayed their latest

drunken brush strokes,
    as if they wore
        the solitary rooms

in which they live. The full
    length mirror reflected
        a few scattered clouds

and doubled an already
    infinite blue,
        which is only

another version of absence,
    and is one explanation,
        why their arms lay across

the glass at either end
    and pressed hard against
        their bodies, as if what

they carried was more
    fragile than anything
        about themselves,

their arms floating
    outside this sky, while
        their shadows stretched

across the sidewalk
    and angled up the sun-
        struck stucco wall.

Sunday
for Bill Palmer

1

At the mouth of Perchy Creek,
where a wing dike shoves
the cutting current
on an outside curve
back into the main river
channel, a mud flat spreads
like a mute tongue
mouthing the tracks
of ducks and raccoons.

Crossing the small delta,
the creek has withered to
a fluttering vein, too narrow
and shallow for our boat
to pass, and as we turn
testing the depth with paddles,
two heron shake loose
from driftwood stranded
high on the bank.

As if our motions are failures
of air rather than water,
we watch their wide gray
wings rise and fall,
like men who throw themselves
forward convinced their
embrace can reach
beyond their arms,
when they are only flying.

fourteen

2

The banks remain solid as any
institution, and shorebirds crowd
the shallows in the shadows
of sandbars. . . . How can a river
close two weeks early, as if it were
scheduled each year, and it is,
but this November the water level,
ruled by floodgates, drops beyond memory.
But what of the river when it opens

itself, pours forth more than we expected
or desired, as once north of a scattering
of threatened houses called Easley,
when I walked a ridge past Indian burial
mounds, and stood on a bluff that was eroded
by an earlier nameless river, that flowed
a hundred feet above this one called
Missouri, that had lost a clear sense

of meandering, and spread two miles
or more over cornfields and roads.
We command spring floods with sandbags
and photographs of roofs slicing the torrent
like the keels of capsized boats, a proof
that we can sail submerged and live.
But now it's time to raise the drought-
drained reservoirs, and God, God-like,
we limit our access, and believe it.

3

Persistent we try again upriver,
and end watching the squat, upside
down flat head of a catfish, wedged
between rocks of the boat ramp,
rocking in the receding waves that
discourages any attempt at our launching.
Two dozen Canada geese have flocked
to the far shore and preen themselves.
until we gather branches stripped

by beaver, and walk along the soft,
dirty sand picking up an empty whiskey
bottle, soda cans, a diesel oil filter,
and missed clay pigeons, and set them
carefully on boulders and logs ringed
by small pools of water, balanced on sticks
we've stuck into the mud, and thrown
the rest on the bank. Hung from
the sky, or stood on its side,

Miro might have looked again along
this shore, but the pistol is aimed,
the twenty guage loaded, and the geese
fly frantically low along the water,
as the first shots ring our ears and echo
off the bluffs. The glass shatters, clay
pigeons explode, cans buckle and fall,
the oil filter spins on its stick,
and even with our misses the mud leaps.

Transmigration

In front of the window, where cardinals
and even a sparrow hawk have died
attempting to fly through, or enter
into the small listless rooms that home
here, not understanding a life defined
and held behind glass, yet you are ready
to leave your body, as they theirs, to be
carried by nearly weightless palms.

Beyond the window there is a Cascade
pass, where you stop and walk away
from the road to undress. Lying down,
you feel the pricking pleasure of pine
needles under back and thigh, an ant
crawling over an ankle, the sky rushing
over your body.

Farther west, there are streets that drop
into the endless vague questions of the sea,
and the small crowded houses pushed back
by their answers. A gull, balanced
on one leg, gives order to refuse
along decaying wharves and oil-stained
beaches, where wet sand remembers equally
kelp, crab shells, and footprints.

Ravens and jays pick through the body
of fog, and you wait to awake from some
terrible dream that hasn't yet happened.
You must be satisfied opening the door,
to be a small background figure merging
with these ghostly birds and their ruinous

cries, that vandalize windows, leaving
their bodies to fly through the grass.

The Old Anxieties

Scattered over sidewalks in June,
acorns smaller than match heads;
shadows of leaves curling into fists,
surrendering to the lightest breeze;
rising ropes of heat and the indelible
streaks of nightcrawlers

on concrete; and fields bleached
beyond themselves, glowing long after
the sun has set; everywhere beginnings
with clearer ends; and still my son
calls to me from the middle of a pond,
where he floats half-submerged

on a half-inflated inner tube, so head
and shoulders are all that greets the heat.
I don't respond, standing on the dock, and he
shouts again. The clatter of cattail blades
fills the gaps between loud words; the sweep
of a dozen swallows tangles above his head;

and his feet continue to slowly tread, refusing
the invitation to quietly escape with nothing
but handfuls of water. Alone in the unblinking,
but shrivelling eye of the pond, he tries
once more, "What's the matter, getting too old?"
I point to the far shore, where a bullfrog

the size of a boat, its head the green of scum,
its body cool as mud, has just let loose
a baritone belch different from the usual
bass rolls, and it comically leaps from side

to side toward higher ground, dragging
a writhing water snake that has bitten one

of its hind legs. I continue to point, but
he can't see what it is through the encircling
surface glare, doesn't care, and wants
to know why I am still on the dock,
as if welded to the heat, and not jumping
into the water.

For Good Reason

SHE insists on a midnight swim
the first weekend in October
nearest her birthday, when frogs
are tentative soloists, the hunched
banks quiet, and the water strangely

empty; and some years, the ones
we can no longer separate, but fuse
into an ache, are warm, and there
is little to say, except perhaps,
once in that stillness with only

her own blood-rush rocking her
in a sanguine autism, she gasped,
as if an unexpected, though not
unwanted hand touched her breast,
swelling her heart to make room

for another year; and beside the dim
outline of willows, and the almost
imperceptible rustle of cattails
and clothes falling around the pale
stem of her body, she stepped

through her breath and down into
the fluid darkness, toes blindly
gripping slippery clay, until deep
enough to stroke, arm over arm,
farther out, following her own

splashing echoes, striking a tinder
of stars, and the chill reflections

twenty-one

firing the foundations of heaven,
currents of earth, and she turned back,
not trusting what she was becoming.

A Brief Note on Principles

1

After a night at a hard birth
when the light dilates in
the window, when what looms
is loss or the beginning
of a long succession of failures,
and the contractions compress
to seconds and sweat, finally
the baby is pulled out, sometimes
destined to carry the forcep's
scars under a strange tangle
of hair, or worse, below the roots
like cattails in a pond where
a bass sculls, a gaudy lure
hooked just below its tailfin
that trails a broken line.

2

And so with a shovel
we walk to the west end
of the garden, where what is
left over, weeded out, raked
up, is rotting, and again,
we hear a soft sound,
the entrance, or the leaving,
leaning the shovel back,
lifting a severed fist
of earth alive with worms;
a body preparing for seed
a grassy placenta.

twenty-three

3

Their soft bodies are threaded
over the barb and down the curve
of the hook, stopping where it turns
up toward the nylon leader. They are
suspended below red and white
bobbers, and when the plastic
float denies the rhythmic push
of wind, sinks and rises, pulls
away, when a life stretches
the line taut, the hook is set
with a jerk of the rod.

Myth leaps above the surface:
was it the glance backwards over
the right shoulder; the striped
shirt unwashed for weeks; standing
sideways downwind; the third cast,
the fourth; or was the bass simply
feeling sentimental, as we sometimes
do pulling pain out of our bodies
like a steel barb when we forgot
the small part of us that drowns
in each breath.

On the reed-choked shore
the body contracts, the ribs
tighten into a stuttering apostrophe
of gasps, the knife slits the belly,
the entrails peel out with a quick
twist of the index finger,
and scraped scales shoot
through the air numerous
and small as stars.

twenty-four

Night Edges

It's late, as it always is,
and no matter how fast I move
along the dry creek bed, the light
is gone, a brief chromatic splash
just beyond the ridge cedars, and now
overhanging branches of birch
and sycamores are a black lace
where a bat weaves.

My pupils swell, as if to challenge
what moves through the starlight
below the meteor's fading scar,
and as if nothing can hurt so much
distance, I quickly wish on its burned
out trail, my head turned up
and straining to see what little
I can, as the painful and exhausted
yelping of coon dogs trails off
down the valley, chained to a scent
that will run them close to death;

and perhaps that is what I hope
to see, and not see an edge of,
yet hear all around: in the splash
in the spring fed pool, the rattle
of rocks on the gravel bar, or something
in the trees, but their direction divides
into three hundred sixty degrees with minutes,
seconds, arcs, and tangents, and it is still
not enough;

and it does no good to sit back in other

hemispheres and look up, knowing
that incendiary flare in one corner of sky
is an eons-old supernova in the Tarantula
Nebula, that light could be so slow,
or this emptiness so large, as last year
on the beach, the moon's reflection
across the water, between sand
and horizon, left nothing joining the earth's
curve to the pregnant sway of moon,
or any sense to gravity, and I started
falling toward that socket of space;
as now, beyond the yellow hem of campfire
stitched against the mud-rooted bank,
a frog calls an ancient rhythm like two
flat stones slowly beat together,
and with the incessant whip-poor-will,
they drag me out of sleep to stare
at the glove of darkness pressing
against my face, an edgeless velvet grip
that holds long after I have risen.

And there are nights I do not want
to be let go, as I lie on my side
propped on one elbow, huddled near
a small bed lamp listening to my son
read of the Civil War, his fascination
with so much death and the peculiar
patterns it forges, and we don't want
to stop with naval engagements, guerrilla
skirmishes, vast battles, and incomprensible
casualties.

In his small circle of light
it is contained, and distant as stars,

whose spasms are too old to hurt,
but it's late, and his mother demands
the light off, so he may fall back
into his own blueprint of night.

Walkabout/Ocean City

It's a good sign that these hard-shelled
insects with their stubborn raspings are here;

but almost no one can hear them in their few
square feet of splotched sand, between foot-long

hot dogs and the high dreamy fluff of cotton
candy; there declaring an uneasy allegiance

with the shadowy silences under miles of boarded
walk fronting surf and jewelry shops, over-priced

shells and fortune tellers, sometimes three
to a tent with tarot, crystal, and palm readings;

and still there's a slow winding line to the future,
as gull on guardrails, or flying overhead,

voice their impatient schedules to the perpetually
moving crowds, out to measure themselves

against another evening; enthralled legions
quickly close ranks as a few strollers fall away

early, weak of heart or simply tired, seeing
the rounded, rotting stumps of wharf pilings

that step off into the sea, each one shorter
than the last until only a turbulent ghostly

foam marks a vanishing, where others once
walked arm-in-arm, tailored and parasoled,

unhurried and leaning on what's not now there,
whispering vows only the sea keeps, but after

the tide pushes closer that bitten wafer of moon,
its gleaming sickle sweeping low, as if harvesting

waves, the children draw back with their skate-
boards and shouts, to temporary homes sur-
    rounded

by smooth pebbled lawns, places where they
    don't
grow old fast enough, and later will always be

caught remembering, where the old linger
on benches backed against a painting of pastel

evenings, listening to the echoes of footfalls
among crickets.

Descendants

1

First one tire leaves the asphalt,
and the ditch opens and the uncut grass
waves inviting us down, but not
really caring one way or the other,

and we chose the other, the steering
wheel lurching as the tires skid
back onto the road, and the trailer
pulling the boat blindly follows

with a jolt, and our hearts, that
we were so unaware of swell,
claiming more room than our bodies,
and beat against the window in their

flight; and if that wasn't enough
after crossing the one lane bridge
over Bonne Femme Creek, we swerve
missing a stopped car, its door

wide open, and the driver standing
behind it half-bent-over staring
at something lying in the gravel,
and this time the truck runs

one wheel into a water filled ditch,
spinning until we are motionless,
listing like the ship we are not,
and though we continue on, four-wheel

drive lifting us out of the mud
and off the axles, we doubt
the final miles, whether we want
to or not.

2

Where the heavy sediment darkened
currents cut away from the limestone
bluffs, away from the railroad tracks
that shadow the south bank, and the stone

and earthen dikes that force it back
away from plowed fields, we sail into
a bouyant flock of migrating Caspian
terns, rising and returning to the roiled

surfaces, running their open scapel-
sharp beaks across the ever slipping
skin of water; terns turning on the arc
of one wing, feathered tops spinning

in the warp and woof of flight,
a candent concatenation whirling
around us, and once through we circle
back, eager to again enter this plumed

swirl, but blending into the riparian
light, appearing over the riotous vined
and foliaged shore, spanning the tumbled
gray riprap reaching out into the river,

a single lustrous black tern glides,
as real and beautiful as the rest.

thirty-one

Final Turns

I've come across an old address
        written in the lower right
hand corner of a page in the middle
        of a spiral notebook full
of accidents:

February 29, the day accountants
        celebrate after all else has failed;
July 20, the heat is oppressive, air-
        conditioners are immortal illusions;
October 15, on the pin oak by the porch
        a leaf moves, nothing less.

I try to recall what it was about
        each change of direction:
after the viaduct, how many stop-
        lights before the bank
on the northeast corner;
        continue west toward
the prairie until cornfields
        claim every angle of vision;
and where a hawk perches
        in the top dead branches
of a black locust, that's as close
        as anyone gets before the wind
picks up shaking loose local
        landmarks.

At noon mirages spill across
        the road; a heat-warped sky
wedged between graveled shoulders.
        This way, pointing over

phantom water, through an azure
        emptiness, not comprehending
the arrival of any horizon,
        any promise.

Then again, it's the warmest year
        on record, the hottest decade,
a single degree higher, which isn't
        much unless it's the earth,
and now the polar ice melts;
        how much, how fast,
and will these low rolling hills
        gather rain, where through
the windshield an instant of ocean
        washes over the evening sky,
waves of blurred light, and flocks
        of blackbirds obscuring
the field's treeline, a feathered
        spray, a tide of wings
settling just west of town.

Nearly there on Route M; left
        on Liberty Lane; stay right
at all forks; turn between the open
        wound of an unfinished house
and parked bulldozer; another turn
        healed by second growth;
and a final turn waiting to be erased.

Relativity

Nothing moves at the same speed scimming
    in a high-powered boat over a wind-
        chopped surface. Winter-bare

birches along the bank splinter in all
    directions as we pass; flocks
        of geese and ducks rise from

backwaters of wingdikes, loudly tying
    and untying themselves until
        they begin to unravel south;

islands blur, and the blowing sand
    is a dry mist hissing as it falls
        into shallows along their shores;

and at the base of one limestone bluff,
    bent between boulders, the dull shine
        of a plane wing.

We watch the channel bouys; stay left
    of the green, right of the red,
        and leave the current behind,

though it is always ahead, and only drift-
    wood and plastic bottles that we pass.
        In an open boat at forty miles per hour

we exchange faces with the wind, but it's
    not enough for this earth to curve any-
        less than it is between Mokane

and the Gasconade River, or the warp of our
skin to slough its shadow and hasten
our acceleration.

Staying in One Place

When we finally know it's not quite
    what we wanted, and no matter how
      long we wait will not be long enough,
that's it, something like the mockingbird

across the yard, in an elm that sprouted
    when we first moved here to build
      this house, the thin trunk now as tall
as the roof gable, and knowing it's a matter

of time, for the tree and the house, and not
    all that much longer, and still
      this bird sings, not a single series
of rising and falling notes that might lead

to some soundless singing edge of self,
    but it vocalizes nearly everything
      it hears, refuses to let go,
as if it had forgotten its own anguished

notes, or lost them among so many, or
    simply become unimportant after
      the passing of whole days and the dark
quarters of night, yet each song

lasts a breath, unlike the rancher over
    the hill to the north, calling his
      cattle to the barn with a low moan,
answered with explosive force by the herd,

and backed by his yelping dog, stepped on
    by a quick turn of hooves, or kicked

for barking, all sounding certain enough
to be just behind the house, while the mocking-

bird, its path across the field marked
    by the staccato white of wingbeats,
    lands on a fencepost, and not giving
up, starts again, as if perched

inside my ear, here on the porch, balanced
    on rotting nylon webbing, the aluminum
    frame of the lawn chair split, where
water seeped and froze a season ago.

Yet Other Waters
for Bobette

> You could not step twice in the same rivers;
> for others and yet other waters . . .
> --Heraclitus

With sand to shake from damp towels;
to work out of our shoes on the porch
step, turning them upside down;

to wash out hair and scalp, the softest
folds of skin; and later to fall
from the novel, its cover slightly

curled from too much sun, and there
on the desk, not to read, but to find
no good reason to continue, seeing each

grain, each rounded edge and prismatic
center, a kaleidoscope of grit to be swept
clean and carried off . . . but then I can't

stop recalling: pulling her close, wet
and naked, chilled by the tidal wind,
nipples puckered, the curve of her spine

drifted with sand, and the waves breaking,
breaking . . . . Is this what
Heraclitus meant, that we could not

step into the same body twice, whether
it is a river, ourselves, or another,
that we are not just the same slipping

away, but the sand we walk over
and carry with us, caught in our cuffs
and shoes, is forever changed,

and changes us, though love may cling
like each grain late in the day
on dunes still leaning against a winded sea.

This first edition of 200 copies of
Walter Bargen's *Yet Other Waters*
was handset in 12 pt. Garamond Old Style
and handfed and printed on a 6 x 10 Kelsey.
Paper is Warren Old Style acid-free paper.
All book design and production was by
Clarence Wolfshohl. Printed
in winter & spring
1989 - 1990
at
Timberline Press,
Fulton, Missouri.